The Sayings of Dorothy Parker

The Sayings of

DOROTHY
PARKER

edited by
S.T. Brownlow

with an introduction by
Antony Rouse

Duckworth

Reprinted 1995, 1996
Second edition February 1995
First published in 1992 by
Gerald Duckworth & Co. Ltd.
The Old Piano Factory
48 Hoxton Square, London N1 6PB
Tel: 071 729 5986
Fax: 071 729 0015

A catalogue record for this book is available
from the British Library

ISBN 0 7156 2677 9

Typeset by Ray Davies
Printed in Great Britain by
Redwood Books Ltd., Trowbridge

Contents

Publisher's Note

Many of Dorothy Parker's witticisms have passed into legend and most of them appear, in one form or another, in the standard biographical compilations. Where versions differ the most plausible has been chosen. Extracts from her written work are referred by page number to *The Collected Dorothy Parker* (Duckworth 1973), a reissue of *The Portable Dorothy Parker* (Viking 1944).

Introduction

by Antony Rouse

'I'm just a little Jewish girl trying to be cute,' Dorothy Parker once said.

It was a half-truth. She was half Jewish.

Dorothy Parker was born in New Jersey on 22 August 1893. Her mother was English-American. Her father, Henry Rothschild, was a prosperous Jewish businessman but no relation of the famous Rothschilds. There were two other children, older than Dorothy by some years. Mrs Rothschild died when Dorothy was seven and was replaced by an unpopular stepmother three years later. Dorothy for some reason left school at fourteen and little is known about the next few years of her life. According to her own account, she just read a lot.

Then, when she was twenty, her father died. He seems to have left little money. At any rate she set out to earn a living. She played the piano for a dancing school. She got a job writing captions for the fashion photographs in *Vogue* and was soon mocking the *Vogue* style. 'There was a little girl who had a little curl, right in the middle of her forehead. When she was good she was very, very good, and when she was bad she wore this divine night-dress of rose-coloured mousseline de soie, trimmed with frothy Valenciennes lace.'

She soon moved to *Vogue*'s new sister, *Vanity Fair*, where she succeeded P.G. Wodehouse as its dramatic critic and along the way married a stockbroker, Edwin Pond Parker II. At about the same time she became the centre of the Algonquin Round Table, a group of young writers and journalists eager for fame who lunched at a large table at the Algonquin Hotel in Manhattan. Among the group was a young journalist on an Army newspaper who had this idea for a magazine. He was called Harold Ross and the magazine was the *New Yorker*, which was to publish much of her work. Another frequenter of the lunches was Franklin Adams, a famous columnist who wrote in the style of Samuel Pepys and spread Dorothy Parker's reputation. 'But I loved Mistress Dorothy Parker the best of any of them,' he wrote of a party, 'and loathe to leave her, which I did not do till near five in the morning, and so home.'

It was at the Algonquin that Dorothy Parker developed her public character. She was one of the boys. She delivered lethal judgments in quiet, formal sentences littered with four-letter words. She partied late into the night. In public her husband, Edwin Parker, was seldom with her because he had little in common with the Round Table wits. In private he drank, and Dorothy started to drink with him. The marriage was soon in trouble and the pair temporarily separated.

With her marriage collapsing, Dorothy Parker began to exercise her talent for picking badly. Her taste in men 'was, indeed, bad, even for writer ladies,' wrote her friend, the playwright Lillian Hellman. Dorothy agreed. 'I require only three things of a man: he must be handsome, ruthless and stupid.' She required therefore that her love affairs should be unhappy. Then she used them in the rueful and cynical verse and the fiction which she published in the 1920s.

In 1927 her first volume of poems, *Enough Rope*, astonishingly became a bestseller and she was famous. And her fame grew with the column she wrote for the *New Yorker* under the pseudonym 'Constant Reader'. The column was not only influential. It was also original, in that she freely admitted both her own prejudices and her own physical or emotional state at the time of writing. Instead of the Olympian judgment, she gave the wry apology. One piece began: 'It is with a deep, though a purely personal, regret that the conductor of this department announces the visitation upon her of a nasty case of the rams.' More than half the ensuing review was a description of her latest hangover.

From her mid-twenties onwards, Dorothy Parker was seldom entirely sober. She was also frequently suicidal. After one affair and an abortion, she tried to cut her wrists. 'Eddie doesn't even have a sharp razor,' she reported. This was the first and probably the most serious of her suicide attempts. It was followed at intervals over the next few years by three others – with veronal, a bottle of shoe polish and barbiturates.

> Razors pain you;
> Rivers are damp;
> Acids stain you;
> And drugs cause cramp.
> Guns aren't lawful;
> Nooses give;
> Gas smells awful;
> You might as well live.

And you might as well live with the rich, who arrived with the fame and invited her to gigantic houses on Long Island furnished with many handsome, stupid and rich young men.

Perhaps escaping to France, like Fitzgerald and Hemingway, would be the answer. It wasn't. After a few months she returned to New York and also divorced her husband. She was now thirty-five and, according to a friend, the men were in and out of her apartment like the mail.

In 1934 she met Alan Campbell, a handsome actor ten years her junior. When he was asked to join a theatre company in Denver, Colorado, for several months, she decided to go with him. The press found them. To avoid scandal, Campbell announced that he and Dorothy were married. Then they married. The marriage seems to have worked well for some years, with Campbell happy to organise her life and she thankful to be organised. Soon after the marriage she stopped writing verse and wrote little fiction. But she also stopped trying to kill herself. The couple moved to Hollywood, hired as a team to write scripts – most notably *A Star is Born*. Script-writing, she said, was 'strenuous boredom'. But she and Campbell were earning a lot of money – $2,000 a week at a time when a typist earned $20. And for one brief, giddy period, Sam Goldwyn was paying them $5,000 a week. 'You're a great poet,' he told her. ' "Men never make a pass at girls wearing eyeglasses." That's a great poem and you wrote it.'

Well, that's the story. And it should be true – as it should be true that she shocked the legal head of MGM by asking 'Where does my contract allow time to fornicate?' During her marriage to Campbell she was twice pregnant and she twice miscarried, and after the second miscarriage the marriage foundered. She and Campbell divorced in 1944, remarried in 1950, separated a year later and lived together again from 1961 until his death from an overdose in 1963.

Her last film work was for a projected Marilyn Monroe movie which was abandoned with Marilyn's death. After Campbell's death she returned to New York and lived in the Volney Hotel, 'the kind of hotel where businessmen install their mothers and then run.' She had, as usual, a dog. She watched a lot of television and apparently admired in particular the BBC satirical programme 'That Was The Week That Was.' She drank a lot. Chaotic with money ('Dot will never be happy until she is on relief,' said one of her lovers), at her death her estate was valued at $20,000. She was 74 years old.

Dorothy Parker wrote no full-length novel, although she tried. A couple of plays were written about her, but her own attempts at play-writing (with collaborators) were not successful. Her reviews of books and theatre are still readable, but no more than that. But her early stories still read fresh today. She took great trouble over them. 'I can't write five words but I change seven,' she once wrote.

She kept her fiction almost free of the destructive wisecrack for which she was famous in conversation, and almost free of the cynicism of her poems. She brought to the *New Yorker* a new kind of short story conducted entirely in dialogue or monologue. In her account of the battle between the sexes, both sides are at fault. If men lack the ability to understand women, then women compound the problem by possessiveness and jealousy. The sexes want different things, so disaster is inevitable. 'Woman lives but in her Lord, Count to ten and man is bored,' she wrote in a poem called 'General Review of the Sex Situation'.

Dorothy Parker's general attitude to the sex situation was that the men had most of the weapons. And her general political attitude was to be on the side of the out-gunned. She visited Spain during the Spanish Civil War, wrote about it and worked raising money for the North American Committee to Aid Spanish Democracy. She may have been a member of the Communist party. She was certainly

for a time sympathetic to Communism.
She supported the formation of a union for
writers in Hollywood. None of her friends
took her political attitudes very seriously.
She outlived almost all of them and left her
estate and any future income from it to
Martin Luther King and the National
Association for the Advancement of
Colored People.

The Sexes

Woman wants monogamy;
Man delights in novelty.
Love is woman's moon and sun;
Man has other forms of fun.
Woman lives but in her lord;
Count to ten, and man is bored.
With this the gist and sum of it,
What earthly good can come of it?
'General review of the sex situation',
CDP, p. 184

By the time you swear you're his,
    Shivering and sighing,
And he vows his passion is
    Infinite, undying –
Lady, make a note of this:
    One of you is lying.
'Unfortunate coincidence',
CDP, p. 149

Lady, lady, should you meet
One whose ways are all discreet,
One who murmurs that his wife
Is the loadstar of his life,
One who keeps assuring you
That he never was untrue,
Never loved another one …
Lady, lady, better run.
'Social note',
CDP, p. 164

Some men break your heart in two,
    Some men fawn and flatter,
Some men never look at you;
    And that clears up the matter.

'Experience',
CDP, p. 187

Let another cross his way
    She's the one will do the weeping!
Little need I fear he'll stray
    Since I have his heart in keeping.

Let another hail him dear –
    Little chance that he'll forget me!
Only need I curse and fear
    Her he loved before he met me.

'Mortal enemy',
CDP, p. 324

They hail you as their morning star
Because you are the way you are.
If you return the sentiment,
They'll try to make you different;
And once they have you safe and sound
They want to change you all around.
Your moods and ways they put a curse on;
They'd make of you another person.
They cannot let you go your gait;
They influence and educate.
They'd alter all that they admired.
They make me sick, they make me tired.

'Men',
CDP, p. 174

'And if he's gone away,' said she,
'Good riddance, if you're asking me.
I'm not a one to lie awake
And weep for anybody's sake.
There's better lads than him about!
I'll wear my buckled slippers out
A-dancing till the break of day.
I'm better off with him away!
And if he never come,' said she,
'Now what on earth is that to me?
I wouldn't have him back!' I hope
Her mother washed her mouth with soap.

'Story',
CDP, p. 341

Oh, there once was a lady, and so I've been
      told,
Whose lover grew weary, whose lover
      grew cold.
'My child,' he remarked, 'though our
      episode ends,
In the manner of men, I suggest we be
      friends.'
And the truest of friends ever after they
      were –
Oh, they lied in their teeth when they told
      me of her!

'Fable',
CDP, p. 320

Should they whisper false of you,
Never trouble to deny;
Should the words they say be true,
Weep and storm and swear they lie.
'Superfluous advice',
CDP, p. 349

Whose love is given over-well
Shall look on Helen's face in hell,
Whilst they whose love is thin and wise
May view John Knox in paradise.
'Partial comfort',
CDP, p. 320

Love is for unlucky folk,
Love is but a curse.
Once there was a heart I broke:
And that, I think, is worse.
CDP, p. 117

Men seldom make passes
At girls who wear glasses.
'News item',
CDP, p. 174

Lips that taste of tears are the best for kissing.

I hate Women. They get on my Nerves.

People

If I had a shiny gun,
I could have a world of fun
Speeding bullets through the brains
Of the folk who give me pains;
Or had I some poison gas,
I could make the moments pass
Bumping off a number of
People whom I do not love.
But I have no lethal weapon –
Thus does Fate our pleasure step on!
So they still are quick and well
Who should be, by rights, in hell.

'Frustration',
CDP, p. 342

To a woman wearing a cape trimmed with monkey fur:

'Really? I thought they were beards.'

To a friend who asked her if she liked her hair:

'Lovely. I can't wait for mine to go gray so I can have it made blue.'

Of Clare Booth Luce, said to be very kind to her inferiors:

'Wherever does she find them?'

Colliding with Clare Booth Luce in a doorway:

CBL: 'Age before beauty.'
DP (stepping aside): 'Pearls before swine.'

Her locks had been so frequently and so drastically brightened and curled that to caress them, one felt, would be rather like running one's fingers through julienne potatoes.

You know, that woman speaks eighteen languages. And she can't say 'No' in any of them.

There were two things that would always bewilder her, she said: how a zipper worked and the exact function of Bernard Baruch.

Challenged to use the word 'horticulture' in a sentence:

'You can lead a whore to culture, but you can't make her think.'

A man once showed a so-called indestructible watch to Benchley and Dorothy Parker. They whammed it against a table-top, and then put it on the floor and stamped on it. The dismayed owner picked it up and put it to his ear. 'It's stopped,' he said incredulously.

Benchley and Parker together: 'Maybe you wound it too tight?'

Never trust a round garter or a Wall Street man.

The ugliest modern gesture – that of a man looking at his wrist-watch!

Talking to a friend about a garrulous bore:

Friend: 'She's so outspoken.'
DP: 'By whom?'

On being told that someone wouldn't hurt a fly:

'Not if it was buttoned up.'

Of trying to talk to someone who kept interrupting:

'Like riding on the Long Island railroad – it gets you nowhere in particular.'

To a supercilious youth who said he 'simply couldn't bear fools':

'How odd. Your mother could apparently.'

At a dinner where Lesbians were seriously discussing the possibility of legal Lesbian marriages:

'Of course you must have legal marriages. The children have to be considered.'

Of the Yale prom:

'If all those sweet young things were laid end to end, I wouldn't be at all surprised.'

'Hazel Morse was a large, fair woman of the type that incites some men when they use the word "blonde" to click their tongues and wag their heads roguishly.'
'Big blonde',
CDP, p. 275

Telegram sent to two friends who had been living together and then got married:

'WHAT'S NEW?'

Animals

To a neighbour who told her her dog was a female:

'I always call dogs "he". It don't do to notice everything.'

Of a mongrel:

'All too obviously, it was the living souvenir of a mother who had never been able to say no.'

Bonne Bouche was all that Mrs Hazelton could ask of a pet. She was tiny, she was noiseless, and she had a real talent for sleeping. Mrs Hazelton loved her truly.

Of her pet dog's mange:

'I suppose he got it from a lamp-post.'

Did you ever realise there are just no dogs in Philadelphia? Oh, what an ugly place.

To a friend who was upset that he had to get rid of his cat:

'Have you tried curiosity?'

Such glorious faith as fills your limpid
    eyes,
Dear little friend of mine, I never knew.
All-innocent are you, and yet all-wise.
(For Heaven's sake, stop worrying that
    shoe!)
You look about, and all you see is fair;
This mighty globe was made for you alone.
Of all the thunderous ages, you're the heir.
(Get off the pillow with that dirty bone!)

A skeptic world you face with steady gaze;
High in young pride you hold your noble
    head,
Gayly you meet the rush of roaring days.
(*Must* you eat puppy biscuit on the bed?)
Lancelike your courage, gleaming swift
    and strong,
Yours is a spirit like a May-day song.
(God help you, if you break the goldfish
    bowl!)

'Whatever is, is good' – your gracious
    creed.
You wear your joy of living like a crown.
Love lights your simplest gift of all – a
    friend.
Your shining loyalty unflecked by doubt
You ask but leave to follow to the end
(Couldn't you wait until I took you out?)
'Verse for a certain dog',
CDP, p. 160

The bird that feeds from off my palm
Is sleek, affectionate, and calm,
But double, to me, is worth the thrush
A-flickering in the elder-bush.

'Ornithology for beginners',
CDP, p. 441

It costs me never a stab nor squirm
To tread by chance upon a worm.
'Aha, my little dear,' I say,
'Your clan will pay me back one day.'

'Thought for a sunshiny morning',
CDP, p. 332

All I say is, nobody has any business to go
around looking like a horse and behaving
as if it were all right. You don't catch
horses going around looking like people,
do you?

'Horsie',
CDP, p. 383

Name of her poodle:
'Cliché.'

Name for a pet parrot:
'Onan' (because he spilled his seed on the
bottom of his cage).

Showbiz

Out in Hollywood, where the streets are paved with Goldwyn, the word 'sophisticated' means, very simply, 'obscene'. A sophisticated story is a dirty story ... a 'sophisticate' means one who dwells in a tower made of a DuPont substitute for ivory and holds a glass of flat champagne in one hand and an album of dirty postcards in the other.

Hollywood smells like a laundry. The beautiful vegetables taste as if they were raised in trunks, and at those wonderful supermarkets you find that the vegetables are all wax. The flowers out there smell like dirty, old dollar bills.

Sure, you make money writing on the coast, and God knows you earn it, but that money is like so much compressed snow. It goes so fast it melts in your hand.

Of the slow pace of work in Hollywood:

'Unless someone comes near my office, I'm going to write MEN on the door.'

John Huston is doing something called, very simply, *The Bible*. Now you must admit that's a big job. I think he's going to stop with Moses because he can't stand another moment – he is playing Moses, you see.

Great actress well away into an account of her early days: 'And there I was, at the Capitol Theater at 10.30 in the morning, walking out on a stage for the first time in my life to face thirty-six hundred people...'

DP: 'How could they do that to you?'

Of a performance by Katherine Hepburn:

'She ran the whole gamut of emotions, from A to B.'

Of an actress who, she was told, had fallen and broken a leg in London:

'Oh, how terrible. She must have done it sliding down a barrister.'

Of a Hollywood neighbour who had had his portrait painted in the nude with outsize genitals:

'It's so real, you almost feel he could speak to you, don't you?'

On writing for the films:

'I don't believe the films have anything to do with writing except in a crossword-puzzle kind of way. Writing a script is drawing together a lot of ends which can be worked into a moving picture.'

To Sam Goldwyn, who asked her at dinner: 'Do you really say all those things which the papers report that you say?'

'Do you?'

To an actor with a large nose and no chin to speak of, who spoke to her of his hopes in Hollywood:

'Oh, they've been *searching* for a new Cary Grant.'

Of an elderly actress who, she was told, was acting in *Camelot*:

'Playing a battlement, no doubt.'

Of a performance by her actor husband, Alan Campbell:

'Like watching a performance that Vassar girls would do, all dressed as men, and you'd expect their hair to fall down any minute.'

Of a somewhat effeminate Hollywood neighbour:

'There he goes, tossing his little Shirley Temple curls.'

Telegram to an actress who finally had her baby after many carefully contrived appearances during her long pregnancy:

'GOOD WORK. WE ALL KNEW YOU HAD IT IN YOU.'

Literary

On the Algonquin Round Table:

'It was no Mermaid Tavern, I can tell you. Just a bunch of loudmouths showing off, saving their gags for days, waiting for a chance to spring them. "Did you hear about my remark?" "Did I tell you what I said?" And everybody hanging around asking "What'd he say? What'd he say?" The whole thing was made up by people who'd never been there. And may I say they're still making it up?'

Leaving her place one day at the Algonquin Round Table:

'Excuse me, I have to go to the bathroom.' (*Pause*.) 'I really have to telephone, but I'm too embarrassed to say so.'

Of her job at *Vanity Fair*:

'My boss is an idiot, and the rest of the staff is four young men who go to pieces easily. Even when they're in the best of health, you have to stand on their insteps to keep them from flying away.'

.

When the *New Yorker* editor, Harold Ross, asked her why she hadn't been to the office during the week to write her usual piece:

'Someone was using the pencil.'

On being told that Harold Ross had called her on her honeymoon demanding belated copy:

'Tell him I've been too fucking busy – or vice versa.'

Certainly nobody wants to complain about sex itself; but I think we all have a legitimate grievance in the fact that, as it is shown in present-day novels, its practitioners are so unmercifully articulate about it … There is no more cruel destroyer of excitement than painstaking detail. Who reads these play-by-play reports of passion responds with much the same thrill as he would experience in looking over the blueprints for some stranger's garage.

Of Margot Asquith's four-volume autobiography:

'The affair between Margot Asquith and Margot Asquith will live as one of the prettiest love stories in all literature.'

Attending a party with Somerset
Maugham at which the guests were asked
to complete nursery rhymes:

SM: Higgledy piggledy, my white hen
    She lays eggs for gentlemen.
DP: You cannot persuade her with gun or
    lariat
    To come across for the proletariat.

I don't read the *New Yorker* much these
days. It always seems to be the same old
story about somebody's childhood in
Pakistan.

Somehow those metaphors got mixed
while my back was turned; but you know
yourself, that is likely to happen to
anybody, and there's little use worrying
about it at this day and date. I have
enough troubles without getting my
forehead all over lines with dithering over
the English language.

The nowadays ruling that no word is
unprintable has, I think, done nothing
whatever for beautiful letters. The short
flat terms used over and over, both in
dialogue and narrative, add neither vigor
nor clarity; the effect is not of shock, but of
something far more dangerous – tedium.

On Thurber:

'These are strange people that Mr Thurber has turned loose upon us. They seem to fall into three classes – the playful, the defeated and the ferocious. All of them have the outer semblance of unbaked cookies; the women are of a dowdiness so overwhelming that it becomes tremendous style. Once a heckler complained that the Thurber women have no sex appeal. "They have for my men," he said.'

Appendicitis is the work of Thew Wright AB, MD, FACS, who has embellished his pages with fascinatingly anatomical illustrations, and has remarked in his dedication, that he endeavors throughout this book to bring an understanding of appendicitis to the laity. And it is really terribly hard to keep from remarking, after studying the pictures, 'That was no laity; that's my wife.'

Theodore Dreiser
Should ought to write nicer.

Of Somerset Maugham:

'That old lady is a crashing bore.'

Of the leading lady at the disappointing dress rehearsal of her play *Close Harmony*:

Producer (*whispering*): 'Don't you think she ought to wear a bra in this scene?'
DP: 'God, no. You've got to have something in the show that moves.'

Of Lou Tellegen's memoirs *Women Have Been Kind*:

'Mr Tellegen's childhood was not a happy one. He was brought up by a somewhat unnecessarily strict tutor who taught him, among other things, "the art of the rapier". (Thank God for that little letter "i".)'

Of a play by Channing Pollock:

'*The House Beautiful* is The Play Lousy.'

I suppose that the fair thing to do is to let the blame for the dullness and the embarrassment of *The Admirable Crichton* rest equally upon the cast and upon Sir J.M. ('Never-Grow-Up') Barrie. It doesn't, I feel, matter. Conciseness is not my gift. All my envy goes to the inspired Mr Walter Winchell, who walked wanly out into the foyer after the third act – there are four and they are long, long acts – and summed up the whole thing in the phrase, 'Well, for Crichton out loud!'

George Reith's *The Art of Successful
Bidding* is well over my head. I can't even
jump for it.

In a shifting, sliding world, it is something
to know that Mr A.A. ('Whimsy-the-Pooh')
Milne stands steady. He may, tease that he
is, delude us into thinking for a while that
he has changed; that we are all grown up
now, and so he may be delicately and even
a little pleasurably weary, in front of us;
and then, suddenly as the roguish sun
darting from the cloud, or the little crocus
popping into bloom, or the ton of coal
clattering down the chute, he is our own
Christopher Robin again, and everything is
hippity-hoppity as of old.

This is how it begins: 'The more it snows,
tiddely-pom –'
    'Tiddely what?' said Piglet. (He took, as
you might say, the very words out of your
correspondent's mouth.) 'Pom,' said Pooh.
'I put that in to make it more hummy.'
    And it is that word 'hummy', my
darlings, that marks the first place in *The
House at Pooh Corner* at which Tonstant
Weader Fwowed up.

Paying her last respects to Scott Fitzgerald as he lay in an undertaker's parlor in Los Angeles, and quoting the words of a mourner at the funeral of Jay Gatsby:

'The poor son-of-a-bitch!'

Hemingway avoids New York, for he has the most valuable asset an artist can possess – the fear of what he knows is bad for him.

Of Scott Fitzgerald and Hemingway:

'Fitzgerald was attractive and sweet and he wanted to be nice – Ernest never wanted to be nice; he just wanted to be worshipped. He was a bore then and he remained so – but the damnedest thing about Scott, he didn't know what was funny.'

At a performance of Louÿs' Aphrodite:

'There is even a brand-new drop-curtain, for the occasion, painted with the mystic letters ΑΦΡΟΔΙΤΗ, which most of the audience take to be the Greek word for "asbestos".'

Ernest Hemingway's definition of courage
– his phrase that, it seems to me, makes
Barrie's 'Courage is immortality' sound
like one of the more treble trillings of
Tinkerbell. Mr Hemingway did not use the
term 'courage'. Ever the euphemist, he
referred to the quality as 'guts', and he was
attributing its possession to an absent
friend.

'Now, just a minute,' somebody said, for
it was one of those argumentative
evenings. 'Listen. Exactly what do you
mean by "guts"?'

'I mean,' Ernest Hemingway said, 'grace
under pressure.'

...So, praise the gods, Catullus is away!
And let me tend you this advice, my dear:
Take any lover that you will, or may,
Except a poet. All of them are queer.
It's just the same – a quarrel or a kiss
Is but a tune to play upon his pipe.
He's always hymning that or wailing this;
Myself, I much prefer the business type.
That thing he wrote, the time the sparrow
 died –
(Oh, most unpleasant – gloomy, tedious
 words!)
I called it sweet, and made believe I cried;
The stupid fool! I've always hated birds.

'A letter from Lesbia',
CDP, p. 452

Authors and actors and artists and such
Never know nothing, and never know
   much.
Sculptors and singers and those of their
   kidney
Tell their affairs from Seattle to Sydney.
Playwrights and poets and such horses'
   necks
Start off from anywhere, end up at sex.
Diarists, critics, and similar roe
Never say nothing, and never say no.
People Who Do Things exceed my
   endurance;
God, for a man that solicits insurance!

'Bohemia',
CDP, p. 326

Say my love is easy had,
   Say I'm bitten raw with pride,
Say I am too often sad –
   Still behold me at your side.
Say I'm neither brave nor young,
   Say I woo and coddle care,
Say the devil touched my tongue –
   Still you have my heart to wear.
But say my verses do not scan,
   And I get me another man!

'Fighting words',
CDP, p. 182

Nickname for Alexander Woollcott's New
York apartment:

'Wit's End.'

On being asked the title of her talk to the Congress of American Writers' poetry session in 1939:

'Sophisticated Verse and *The Hell with it*.'

The Lives and Times of John Keats, Percy Bysshe Shelley, and George Gordon Noel, Lord Byron

Byron and Shelley and Keats
Were a trio of lyrical treats.
The forehead of Shelley was cluttered with
    curls,
And Keats never was a descendant of earls,
And Byron walked out with a number of
    girls,
But it didn't impair the poetical feats
Of Byron and Shelley,
Of Byron and Shelley,
Of Byron and Shelley and Keats.

Oscar Wilde

If, with the literate, I am
Impelled to try an epigram,
I never seek to take the credit;
We all assume that Oscar said it.

Harriet Beecher Stowe

The pure and worthy Mrs Stowe
Is one we all are proud to know
As mother, wife, and authoress –
Thank God, I am content with less!

D.G. Rossetti

Dante Gabriel Rossetti
Buried all of his libretti
Thought the matter over – then
Went and dug them up again.

Thomas Carlyle

Carlyle combined the lit'ry life
With throwing teacups at his wife,
Remarking, rather testily,
'Oh, stop your dodging, Mrs C!'

Charles Dickens

Who call him spurious and shoddy
Shall do it o'er my lifeless body.
I heartily invite such birds
To come outside and say those words!

Alexandre Dumas and his son

Although I work, and seldom cease,
At Dumas *père* and Dumas *fils*,
Alas, I cannot make me care
For Dumas *fils* and Dumas *père*.

Alfred, Lord Tennyson

Should Heaven send me any son,
I hope he's not like Tennyson.
I'd rather have him play a fiddle
Than rise and bow and speak an idyll.

George Gissing

When I admit neglect of Gissing,
They say I don't know what I'm missing.
Until their arguments are subtler,
I think I'll stick to Samuel Butler.

Walter Savage Landor

Upon the work of Walter Landor
I am unfit to write with candor.
If you can read it, well and good;
But as for me, I never could.

George Sand

What time the gifted lady took
Away from paper, pen, and book,
She spent in amorous dalliance
(They do those things so well in France).

'A pig's eye view of literature',
CDP, pp. 321-3

Politics

On hearing that President Calvin Coolidge had died:

'How could they tell?'

Of the 1930s:

'They were progressive days. We thought we were going to make the world better – I forget why we thought it, but we did.'

Anything that makes Mussolini sore is velvet so far as I am concerned. If only I had a private income, I would drop everything right now, and devote the scant remainder of my days to teasing the Dictator of All Italy ... Indeed my dream-life is largely made up of scenes in which I say to him, 'Oh, Il Duce – yourself, you big stiff', and thus leave him crushed to a pulp.

He's really awfully fond of coloured people. Well, he says himself, he wouldn't have white servants.

'Arrangement in black and white',
CDP, p. 42

I am not a member of any political party. The only group I have ever been affiliated with is that not especially brave little band that hid its nakedness of heart and mind under the out-of-date garment of a sense of humor. I heard someone say, and so I said it too, that ridicule is the most effective weapon. I don't suppose I ever really believed it, but it was easy and comforting, and so I said it. Well, now I know. I know that there are things that never have been funny, and never will be. And I know that ridicule may be a shield, but it is not a weapon.

Herself

On her young days:

'I was following in the exquisite footsteps of Miss Edna St Vincent Millay, unhappily in my own horrible sneakers … just a little Jewish girl trying to be cute.'

On the Blessed Sacrament Convent, where she was at school:

'It was practically around the corner and you didn't have to cross any avenues, whatever that means. Never mind you couldn't learn anything.'

On her reception there:

'Well, how do you *expect* them to treat a kid who saw fit to refer to the Immaculate Conception as "Spontaneous Combustion"? Boy, did I think I was smart! Still do.'

On the other children:

'They weren't exactly your starched-crinoline set, you know. Dowdiest little bunch you ever saw.'

Of her father:

'On Sundays he'd take us on an outing.
Some outing. We'd go to the cemetery to
visit my mother's grave. All of us,
including the second wife. That was his
idea of a treat. Whenever he'd hear a
crunch of gravel that meant an audience
approaching, out would come the biggest
handkerchief you ever saw and, in a
lachrymose voice that had remarkable
carrying power, he'd start wailing, "We're
all here, Eliza! I'm here. Dottie's here. Mrs
Rothschild is here …".'

Of her stepmother:

'She was crazy with religion. I'd come in
from school and she'd greet me with "Did
you love Jesus today?" Now, how do you
answer that? She was hurt because the
older ones called her "Mrs Rothschild".
What else? That was her name. I didn't call
her anything. "Hey, you", was about the
best I could do.'

Of the servants:

'In those days they used to go down to
Ellis Island and bring them, still bleeding,
home to do the laundry. You know that
didn't encourage them to behave well.
Honest, it didn't.'

Of her mother-in-law:

'She exudes that particular odour of Djer Kiss face powder and dried perspiration that characterises the Southern gentlewoman. She is the only woman I know who pronounces the word "egg" with three syllables.'

To Edmund Wilson:

'I am cheap – you know that.'

Helen of Troy had a wandering glance;
    Sappho's restriction was only the sky;
Ninon was ever the chatter of France;
    But oh, what a good girl am I!
        'Words of comfort to be scratched on a mirror',
            CDP, p. 173

Why would anybody choose a career?

There's little in taking or giving
    There's little in water or wine;
This living, this living, this living
    Was never a project of mine.
            'Coda',
            CDP, p. 357

I was the toast of two continents:
Greenland and Australia.

They say of me, and so they should
It's doubtful if I come to good.
I see acquaintances and friends
Accumulating dividends
And making enviable names
In science, art and parlour games.
But I, despite expert advice,
Keep doing things I think are nice,
And though to good I never come
Inseparable my nose and thumb!
'Neither bloody nor bowed',
CDP, p. 188

Four be the things I am wiser to know:
Idleness, sorrow, a friend, and a foe.

Four be the things I'd been better without:
Love, curiosity, freckles, and doubt.

Three be the things I shall never attain:
Envy, content, and sufficient champagne.

Three be the things I shall have till I die:
Laughter and hope and a sock in the eye.
'Inventory',
CDP, p. 150

There always must be some kind of hitch.
Isn't nature (finish this line for yourself
and get a year's subscription to the *Boston
Post*).

If I don't drive around the park,
I'm pretty sure to make my mark.
If I'm in bed each night by ten,
I may get back my looks again.
If I abstain from fun and such,
I'll probably amount to much;
But I shall stay the way I am,
Because I do not give a damn.

'Observation',
CDP, p. 179

Travel, trouble, music, art
    A kiss, a frock, a rhyme –
I never said they feed my heart
    But still they pass the time.

'Faute de mieux',
CDP, p. 173

To the suggestion that she might start on
her autobiography:

'I'd never be able to do it, but I wish to
God I could! I'd like to write the damned
thing, just so I could call it *Mongrel*!'

Of her supersophisticated New York days:

'We were gallant, hardriding and careless
of life. We were little black eyes that had
gone astray … a sort of Ladies' Auxiliary
of the Legion of the Damned.'

On considering two plays, each containing a character based on her, one by George Oppenheimer and the other by Ruth Gordon:

'I wanted to write my autobiography but now I'm afraid to. George Oppenheimer and Ruth Gordon would sue me for plagiarism.'

When asked by a woman sitting next to her at a first night, 'Are you Dorothy Parker?':

'Yes, do you mind?'

Every love's the love before
    In a duller dress.
That's the measure of my lore –
    Here's my bitterness:
Would I knew a little more,
    Or very much less!

'Summary',
CDP, p. 460

Oh, is it, then, Utopian
To hope that I may meet a man
Who'll not relate, in accents suave,
The tales of girls he used to have?

'De profundis',
CDP, p. 154

I do not like my state of mind;
I'm bitter, querulous, unkind.
I hate my legs, I hate my hands,
I do not yearn for lovelier lands.
I dread the dawn's recurrent light;
I hate to go to bed at night.
I snoot at simple, earnest folk.
I cannot take the gentlest joke.
I find no peace in paint or type.
My world is but a lot of tripe.
I'm disillusioned, empty-breasted.
For what I think, I'd be arrested.
I am not sick, I am not well.
My quondam dreams are shot to hell.
My soul is crushed, my spirit sore;
I do not like me any more.
I cavil, quarrel, grumble, grouse.
I ponder on the narrow house.
I shudder at the thought of men ...
I'm due to fall in love again.

'Symptom recital',
CDP, p. 180

Why is it, when I am in Rome,
I'd give an eye to be at home,
But when on native earth I be,
My soul is sick for Italy?
And why with you, my love, my lord,
Am I spectacularly bored,
Yet do you up and leave me – then
I scream to have you back again?

'On being a woman',
CDP, p. 334

The ladies men admire, I've heard,
Would shudder at a wicked word.
Their candle gives a single light;
They'd rather stay at home at night.
They do not keep awake till three,
Nor read erotic poetry.
They never sanction the impure,
Nor recognise an overture.
They shrink from powders and from
    paints.
So far, I have had no complaints.

'Interview',
CDP, p. 187

On her pregnancy:

'It serves me right for putting all my eggs
in one bastard.'

Oh, life is a glorious cycle of song,
A medley of extemporanea;
And love is a thing that can never go
    wrong,
And I am Marie of Roumania.

'Comment',
CDP, p. 149

Oh, seek, my love, your newer way;
I'll not be left in sorrow.
So long as I have yesterday,
Go rake your damned tomorrow!

'Godspeed',
CDP, p. 161

Oh, gallant was the first love, and
    glittering and fine;
The second love was water, in a clear
    white cup;
The third love was his, and the fourth was
    mine;
And after that, I always get them all
    mixed up.
'Pictures in the smoke',
CDP, p. 184

For this my mother wrapped me warm,
And called me home against the storm,
And coaxed my infant nights to quiet,
And gave me roughage in my diet,
And tucked me in my bed at eight,
And clipped my hair, and marked my
    weight,
And watched me as I sat and stood:
That I might grow to womanhood
To hear a whistle and drop my wits
And break my heart to clattering bits.
'Fulfilment',
CDP, p. 331

I require only three things of a man: he
must be handsome, ruthless, and stupid.

After a quarrel with John McClain, one of
her handsomer young lovers:

'Yes, his body went to his head.'

Introducing her first husband:

'I want you to meet my little husband.'

Of her second husband:

'Oh, don't worry about Alan. Alan will always land on somebody's feet.'

The sun's gone dim, and
   The moon's turned black;
For I loved him, and
   He didn't love back.
> 'Two volume novel',
> *CDP*, p. 355

In youth, it was a way I had
   To do my best to please,
And change, with every passing lad,
   To suit his theories.
But now I know the things I know,
   And do the things I do;
And if you do not like me so,
   To hell, my love, with you!
> 'Indian summer',
> *CDP*, p. 170

On hearing the door bell or telephone ringing:

'What fresh hell is this?

... Princes, never I'd give offense,
Won't you think of me tenderly?
Here's my strength and my weakness,
    gents –
I loved them until they loved me.

'Ballade at thirty-five',
CDP, p. 167

... Why is it no one ever sent me yet
    One perfect limousine, do you suppose?
Ah no, it's always just my luck to get
    One perfect rose.

CDP, p. 165

It's not the tragedies that trick us. It's the
messes. I can't stand messes.

On being told at a Halloween party that
people were ducking for apples:

'There, but for a single consonant, is the
story of my life.'

I should have stayed home for dinner. I
could have had something on a tray. The
head of John the Baptist, or something.

Of Elmer Rice:

'Without question the worst fuck I ever had.'

Marriage & Divorce

Accursed from their birth they be
Who seek to find monogamy,
Pursuing it from bed to bed –
I think they would be better dead.

'Reuben's children'
CDP, p. 315

To someone who congratulated her with
the words 'What are you complaining
about? You're married to a charming,
handsome man who adores you. What
more do you want?'

'Presents.'

At the reception following the ceremony of
her remarriage to Alan Campbell:

'People who haven't talked to each other
for years are on speaking terms again
today – including the bride and groom.'

To a cabbie who said he was engaged:

'Then be happy.'

You can get divorced in Connecticut for roller-skating.

Conversation with a so-called friend as they carried out the body of Alan Campbell, who had committed suicide:

Friend: 'Dottie dear, tell me what I can do for you?'

DP: 'Get me a new husband.'

Friend (after a pause): 'I think that is the most callous and disgusting remark I ever heard in my life.'

DP (sighing): 'So sorry. Then run down to the corner and get me a ham and cheese on rye and tell them to hold the mayo.'

Drink & Sleep

On being warned by her doctor that if she didn't stop drinking she would be dead within a month:

'Promises, promises!'

On being asked if she was going to join Alcoholics Anonymous:

'Certainly not. They'd want me to stop now.'

Three highballs, and I think I'm St Francis of Assisi.
'Just the little one',
CDP, p. 360

No more my little song comes back;
    And now of nights I lay
My head on down, to watch the black
    And wait the unfailing gray.
Oh, sad are winter nights, and slow;
    And sad's a song that's dumb;
And sad it is to lie and know
    Another dawn will come.
'The small hours',
CDP, p. 114

I really can't be expected to drop everything and start counting sheep at my age. I hate sheep.
'The little hours',
CDP, p. 378

Houses & Hotels

William Randolph Hearst, who lived with
the movie star Marion Davies in his lavish
turreted mansion San Simeon, at which
Hollywood personalities were frequent
guests, was a strict host. In spite of his own
irregular association, he decreed that no
unmarried couples should sleep together.
When DP broke the rule and was asked to
leave she left the following lines in the
visitors' book:

> Upon my honor
> I saw a madonna
> Standing in a niche
> Above the door
> Of the famous whore
> Of a prominent son of a bitch.

[DP denied this story, saying that she
would never dream of rhyming 'honor'
with 'madonna'.]

Do you know what they do when you die
in this hotel? They used to take them down
on the big elevator in the back, but it's not
running, and they take them down that
front elevator, and you know how small it
is. They have to stand you up.

Of the Volney Hotel in New York, where she had an apartment:

'The kind of hotel where businessmen instal their mothers and then run.'

Women who live alone in small residential hotels throughout the United States have plenty of money and plenty of time: their only occupation is to spend one and kill the other.

On finding herself a guest at a private house:

'I knew it would be terrible. Only I didn't think it would be as bad as this. This isn't just plain terrible; this is fancy.'

On seeing a worn-out toothbrush in their hostess's bathroom:

Fellow guest: 'Whatever do you think she does with that?'
DP: 'I think she rides it on Halloween.'

Death

Time doth flit,
Oh shit!

Promise me that my gravestone will carry
only these words:

'If you can read this you've come too close.'

Razors pain you;
   Rivers are damp;
Acids stain you;
   And drugs cause cramp.
Guns aren't lawful;
   Nooses give;
Gas smells awful;
   You might as well live.

'Résumé',
CDP, p. 154

I never see that prettiest thing –
A cherry bough gone white with spring –
But what I think, 'How gay 'twould be
To hang me from a flowering tree.'

'Cherry white',
CDP, p. 435

If wild my breast and sore my pride,
I bask in dreams of suicide;
If cool my heart and high my head,
I think, 'How lucky are the dead!'

'Rhyme against living',
CDP, p. 435

Drink and dance and laugh and lie
    Love, the reeling midnight through,
For tomorrow we shall die!
    (But, alas, we never do.)

'The flaw in paganism',
CDP, p. 433

Isn't it a bit presumptuous of us to be alive
now that Mr Benchley is dead?

Tombstones in the starlight

1. *The minor poet*
His little trills and chirpings were his best.
No music like the nightingale's was born
Within his throat; but he, too, laid his
    breast
Upon a thorn.

2. *The pretty lady*
She hated bleak and wintry things alone.
All that was warm and quick, she loved
    too well –
A light, a flame, a heart against her own;
    It is forever bitter cold, in Hell.

3. *The very rich man*
He'd have the best and that was none too
    good;
No barrier could hold, before his terms.
He lies below, correct in cypress wood,
And entertains the most exclusive worms.

4. *The fisherwoman*
The man she had was kind and clean
And well enough for every day,
But, oh, dear friends, you should have seen
The one that got away!

5. *The crusader*
Arrived in Heaven, when his sands were
    run,
He seized a quill, and sat him down to tell
The local press that something should be
    done
About that noisy nuisance, Gabriel.

6. *The actress*
Her name, cut clear upon this marble cross,
Shines, as it shone when she was still on
    earth;
While tenderly the mild, agreeable moss
Obscures the figures of her date of birth.
CDP, pp. 438-9

People ought to be one of two things,
young or old. No – what's the use of
fooling? People ought to be one of two
things, young or dead.

You will be frail and musty
With peering, furtive head,
While I am young and lusty
Among the roaring dead

'Braggart',
CDP, p. 127

Her own epitaph:

Excuse My Dust.